# The Truth About Hypnosis and Levels of Consciousness

# The Truth About Hypnosis and Levels of Consciousness

Clyde N. Hollars

**To order additional copies of this book, contact:**
Xlibris Corporation
1-888-795-4274
www.Xlibris.com
Orders@Xlibris.com
95011

# Contents

Chapter 5

Chapter 6

Chapter 7

# Chapter 1

## *Introduction*

While I was in the navy, I was stationed with a chief petty officer who put on a demonstration of hypnosis. He hypnotized some of my friends, and I realized that hypnosis was valid. I always was interested in hypnosis, and learning hypnosis was something that I had to do, I didn't have a choice. I learned how to hypnotize people while I was in the service, and after retiring I became a medical hypnotist and learned about the workings of the mind through the use of hypnosis and found that I had a natural ability to help people.

I graduated from the College of Emotional Consultants, and I worked in a medical clinic doing consultancy and hypnotherapy for several years. You have to trust me when I state that all the following information during hypnotic sessions actually happened.

My research into the information concerning hypnotism made me realize that there is misinformation published in most of the books and other areas being given to the general public. The primary reason for writing this book is to tell the truth about the dangers and possible misuse of hypnotism, so you can still use it and protect yourself.

It is dangerous to tell the truth about hypnosis because this could cause unscrupulous persons to become involved in its use, but this information will allow persons who want to be hypnotized to protect themselves.

The practice of hypnosis requires an understanding of how the human mind works. If you get confused while reading about how the mind works while reading the Truth about Hypnotism, read chapter 5 of the "Levels of Consciousness."

I was going to put "Levels of Consciousness" first, but I feel that "The Truth about Hypnosis" was more important because of the misinformation about it.

"The Levels of Consciousness" attempts to explain this by dividing the mind into three states of consciousness: the soul, the subconscious, and the conscious. Levels of consciousness are based on the information I was given the privilege to experience during my work with subjects during hypnotic sessions. The information is based on sixty years of experience in the use of hypnotism.

I started doing hypnosis in the navy. After I retired, I became a hypnotist in a medical clinic treating patients to overcome psychosomatic disorders. Since retiring, I have continued doing hypnosis and have continued to study how the mind works. I worked with subjects to help them overcome problems that were interfering with their lives. Some of these problems were created in past lives and were influencing them through the subconscious. I also did emotional and family counseling for those who didn't need hypnotherapy.

The medical clinic I worked at had two doctors with two nurses and one nurse to assist me. In my part of the clinic was a well-equipped office, five treatment rooms with a recliner, a tape recorder, earphones, and a chair for me. All rooms had TV cameras connected to a central control room with a TV monitor for each treatment room.

The presence of a nurse or other person can have an inhibiting effect on a subject. The camera is for the protection for both the hypnotist and the subject.

After the initial interview, I made treatment tapes for each patient and updated them as necessary; this allowed me to treat and monitor five subjects at a time.

The term "subject" is just used to identify a person and in no way intended to suggest that they were subject to me.

## Definitions

*Hypnotist:* The person doing the hypnosis.

*Subject(s):* The person(s) being hypnotized.

*Commands:* The commands given by the hypnotists to the subjects.

Depending on the depth of sleep, commands may have become less effective over a period of time and have to be repeated.

*Depth of Sleep:* There is an infinite number of depths. The deepest state of sleep is called somnambulistic state. In this state, a subject will follow all commands.

*Posthypnotic Commands:* The commands given to a subject to be carried out after they have been awakened. Subjects may be instructed to do things that will help resolve their problems. Over time, commands may weaken and have to be reinforced.

*Triggers:* A word, signal, or sound to start an action or thought. It works like the trigger on a gun to cause something to happen in the mind.

This was not written to frighten anyone away from hypnosis but to make you aware that like everything else, it can be misused. Before I tell you of all the dangers of hypnosis, I will say this, under the right conditions, it can be used to successfully treat a large area of emotional, mental, and physical disorders that fall between a medical doctor's knowledge and expertise and the treatment you may receive from a psychiatrist. I will include examples to illustrate how it related to a particular problem with a subject.

## Dangers of Hypnosis

When you are in a hypnotic sleep, you must assume that you are giving the hypnotist total control of your mind and body. In the deepest state of sleep called somnambulistic state, you can be commanded that you will not even remember ever being hypnotized or who hypnotized you. You will not know how deep of a sleep you are going to go into.

The hypnotist can control your mind, your beliefs, your emotions, your likes and dislikes, your fear, your love, your hate, everything. He can control all of your five senses: sight, hearing, touch, smell, and taste. He can change all of these by the snap of the fingers or by some other triggers he installed in your mind.

The following will explain how you can be controlled. He can say, "At the snap of my fingers, you will obey all my commands," such as "When I snap my fingers you will see a large, friendly rabbit sitting next to you. He will not hurt you, you will think he is cute, and you may talk to him. You can hear his little funny voice and may touch his soft fur. You can smell his breath, and it smells like he has been eating a lemon. This makes you taste the lemon, and it makes your mouth start to water. If you don't like that smell, you may change it to the smell of roses by snapping your fingers." All of these things will happen.

## Total Control Means Total Control

The more intelligent a person is, the better subject he makes. Some people may appear to be mentally handicapped, but they may still have tremendous strength of mind but may just lack conscious control; the hypnotist may be able to provide the control.

You have to be very careful when putting a person of extremely high intelligence to sleep because of their ability to concentrate, and their strength of mind can make it difficult to remove commands. If you are easy to be hypnotized, you are not stupid or weak willed as some would have you think. A large percentage of people are very easily influenced to do different things; this is called *being suggestible*, and they are very easy to be persuaded to do almost anything. These persons are also easy to be hypnotized. This condition is usually caused by overdictatorial parents who train a child to do everything they are told to do.

All hypnotic sessions should be recorded on your own camcorder. A record will protect both you and the hypnotist. Take someone you can trust to the sessions, and they can operate your camcorder. If the hypnotist objects to this, it's time to leave. Know that he is recording everything. This record can be reviewed to identify any new problems that may have been caused by the hypnosis.

In the initial interview, the hypnotist may test you to see if you are a good hypnotic subject; if you are, he can implant a command in your mind that "after I wake you up, you will *want* to be hypnotized and will obey all my commands."

A hypnotist can avoid most of the dangers listed if he properly prepares a subject and gives the necessary commands to protect him. Such a command might be "None of the commands or suggestions I give you can ever hurt you, and your mind will automatically reject any and all such commands."

Hypnosis is done verbally, and there is no need for a hypnotist to touch a subject's body unless they require physical assistance getting down and up in a chair or on a couch.

Many books are written by quoting other books on hypnotism. The real danger is that incorrect statements are repeated over into other books. To be fair to other hypnotists, very few use it to resolve physiological problems; most use it for entertainment or to remove bad habits such as smoking.

The following information illustrates some of the information in books and advertisements that are misleading with a play on words, misinformation, or lack of knowledge.

It has been stated that a subject could come out of hypnosis anytime he *wants to* and would not do anything that he doesn't *want to* do. The trick words are *want to*. A hypnotist can give a subject a command that he will *want to* remain asleep and not to awaken until commanded to do so, and he will stay asleep. Understand that the "*wants*" you feel may not all come from your own true desires and may have been planted there. Commercials use these techniques all the time.

A hypnotist can use the strength of your mind against itself and tell a subject that the harder you try to wake up, the deeper asleep you will go. Some subjects have been kept under hypnosis for months. Another wrote that you wouldn't do anything that you wouldn't do in a normal waking state.

*A hypnotic trance is not a normal waking state.*

In the normal waking state, the conscious mind acts as a guard or filter that may prevent you from doing something wrong; but in a trance, the conscious mind is asleep and can't protect you.

Recently, I read an ad in the newspaper which stated, "There is no surrender of mind or control. Anyone can emerge from hypnosis at any time during a session." This hypnotist doesn't know what he's doing or is lying to the public. This can only happen if he has told you it will happen.

A hypnotist can plant a command into the subconscious that "you will *want to* come back for further treatments," and this will ensure that you keep coming back. After you have been hypnotized and you realize that you are acting differently, such as feeling you have to go to see the hypnotist again and again or sending him money or buying him presents or feeling unnatural feelings of affection, protect yourself and review your recordings of the sessions. These compulsions will become less over time.

After being awakened, a subject can still be under the control of the hypnotist for several hours, so it is very important to protect yourself during this period. The length of time depends on how deep the state of sleep you were able to attain.

A hypnotist can get involved in all areas of your mind, but you may not want that done. It is of the utmost importance that the hypnotist understands what you want to be treated for and treats you for only that. Don't agree to hypnotism unless all your questions have been answered to your satisfaction; if not, go some place else.

When looking for a hypnotist, start by asking people who have been hypnotized by that hypnotist and ask the hypnotist a lot of questions and observe his reactions. If he appears less than completely open and honest with you, *leave.*

Remember, just because a person wears a white coat and works in a hospital or clinic doesn't mean that he is an experienced hypnotist, doctor, or therapist. For a small fee you can get certified for whatever you want to be.

The hypnotist and the subject's mind become very closely bonded, possibly one of the closest mental relationships the subject will ever experience with anyone. A side effect of being hypnotized is that the subject may start to identify and bond with the hypnotist and can be easily hypnotized by that person again.

A hypnotist should command a subject, saying, "After I wake you up, you will not respond to any signal, sign, or anything I might say or do and will be normal in every way. You will follow the instructions given to help you. No one will ever hypnotize you again without your expressed permission."

Hypnotists have to be very careful not to betray the subject's trust. Some hypnotists might fall into a trap that has been wittingly or unwittingly set up by their mind or the subject's mind, and they can become romantically involved. The hypnotist also has to be protected from his own and the subject's temptations to do something that might be harmful or illegal. That's what the camcorders are for.

Some hypnotists' egos let them believe that they are just great lovers; the truth is, those romantic feelings are just a reaction to hypnosis. The feelings of affection that occur have to be worked through by the hypnotist; and if handled in the right way, he will become regarded as a trusted and respected figure of authority to the subject.

Total control of another human can be very dangerous. I would be the first to admit that being a hypnotist is a huge ego trip, and being in total control of someone is very exciting. It also carries a great responsibility.

The subjects are paying you to do a job, not to take advantage of them even if they feel and you know that they want to be taken advantage of. If something happened to the hypnotist or an emergency occurred and the subject is left unattended, the subconscious should take over and wake you or you can go into a normal sleep and wake up. This doesn't always happen, and the hypnotist should protect the subject from this by commanding the subject to immediately wake up if left unattended or when an emergency occurs.

Hypnosis is not a fun entertainment as you may have seen in stage shows. It can be dangerous when used by an unscrupulous person. What a volunteer subject sees and feels under hypnosis may be funny to an audience but is very real to them.

In London, a woman won a lawsuit against a stage hypnotist. (A stage hypnotist is one who hypnotizes for entertainment.) Apparently, she was regressed to a period when she was eight years old and relived a traumatic incident of sexual abuse by an uncle. The hypnotist could have removed that incident from her mind. He brought it into her conscious mind and left it where it became a problem causing panic attacks, depression, and attempts of suicide.

A subject, while under hypnosis, can be put into a state where he will appear to be fully awake, talk to, and answer all questions from the persons present and still remain under control of the hypnotist.

I should also tell you that the control of a subject can be turned over to someone else. Isn't that just wonderful? No! It's not and should never be done except in an extreme emergency. I don't want someone else to even touch one of my subjects.

## Religion and Hypnosis

If you are not a religious person before you become a hypnotist, you most likely will develop a religious philosophy before long. You have to be knowledgeable of the prevailing religions in the area that you're subjects live.

A tremendous number of the subject's problems are related to religion and the related conflicts between what they are told, what they desire, and the hypocrisies that they see being practiced by the church authorities and the members of the congregation as well as their own families.

The hippies of the fifties and sixties ran head-on with the church and state authorities and their own parents when they started to practice what they had been told to do during bible study. (Don't kill, love one another, live as the flowers, don't work, etc., etc.) They were a big threat because this was new, and authorities didn't know how to handle the situation. Anything that threatens the prevailing power structure will be attacked and distorted, of course, all in the name of God and law and order. This should remind parents not to let someone teach a child things they don't want that child to do.

If I sound antireligious, let me assure you I'm not; but I don't have a lot of respect for any organization's leaders who misuse their trust and teach fear or take advantage of their position. Religious organizations can intentionally or unintentionally use hypnosis. It would be relatively easy to start a religious organization using hypnosis.

I visited a church that openly used hypnosis in their services. Whoever organized it knew what they were doing. The man conducting the service was very presentable and had a wonderful voice and personality. The facilities were impressive and had some of the best music, sound equipment, decorations and lighting appropriate to the use of hypnosis and had several women on its staff. They were the friendliest group you would ever want to meet.

They also sold books on mind control and hypnotism. I don't know if this organization misused hypnosis, but if they wanted to, there are no laws to stop them. There are thousands of religious cults that brainwash their followers with drugs, alcohol, sex, fear, mass hypnosis, and false promises of heaven and paradise. Some have to be kidnapped from the cults and kept locked up to be deprogrammed. All these things can be done under the protection of our constitution under free speech. It can take a long time to deprogram their minds. Some can't be deprogrammed because they have been brainwashed so completely to believe that's what they *want to* do.

When children's consciousness is being developed, it's their parent's responsibility to provide them with the information and protection they need. No one ever said that it's easy being a parent. Do not let yourself or your children be consulted by an individual consultant/therapist in a private, one-on-one basis such as hypnosis, religion, or professional organizations. This is especially important in situations dealing with the emotions.

Parents are responsible to protect their children, 365 days a year, 24 hours a day, 7 days a week. They must know who their friends are, where they are, whom they are with, and what they are doing. You must inspect their rooms and cars. This is known as "tough love" because it's tough on the parents. Forget about not trusting them until they earn that trust. You cannot turn that responsibility over to any one else. They may think they hate you; but eventually, after they see the trouble their friends get into, they will understand that you were trying to protect them.

One mother brought her young daughter in because the girl was letting her boyfriend slip in through the window, and the girl got pregnant. There wasn't much I could do for her except send her up to see the doctors. They arranged for an abortion. They put her on birth control pills, but six months later the girl came back, and she was pregnant again. She forgot to take her pills. I asked where her mother was, and she said she was out in the car. I told the girl to go up front and watch TV. I went out and got the mother to come in and told her that the only way that the girl could be kept from becoming pregnant was to have the tubes tied. The mother had done all she could do. I don't know what the mother finally did.

Ugly is only skin deep, but stupidity goes all the way to the bone. There are things that hypnosis can't help.

# Chapter 2

## *Psychosomatic Disorders*

Psychosomatic disorders are a group of mental and physical disorders of presumably psychogenesis in origin. For a list of these disorders, see the *Diagnostic and Statistical Manual of Mental Disorders* published by the American Psychiatric Association. This group of disorders is characterized by physical symptoms that are caused by suppressed emotional factors and involves a single organ system, usually under the autonomic nervous system innervations. The individual my not be consciously aware of their emotional state.

There are nine categories of disorders listed: skin, musculoskeletal, tension headaches, respiratory, cardiovascular, hemic and lymphatic, gastrointestinal, gento-urinary, and endocrine sense organs. These disorders are usually caused by suppressed emotional factors. They can be treated by hypnosis, and the mental and physical symptoms may be removed.

The following are some of the ones that cause us problems:

*Minor problems:*

- The involuntary twitching of muscles.
- Biting the fingernails
  * Stuttering
- Dizziness
- Overeating
- Under eating

*Major problems*:

- Migraine Headaches
- Schizophrenia (splitting personality)

- Masochism
- Alcoholism
- Drug Dependence
- Suicide

The following information contain examples of actual cases to help illustrate a particular problem. Their names are not used to protect their privacy.

A subject came in who was hallucinating and said that his mother was trying to control him using extrasensatory perception methods (ESP). He was taking several mind-altering drugs, including LSD. He was trying to destroy his mother with mind control. He seemed to have lost conscious control and was operating out of his subconscious because of the drugs.

He responded well to hypnosis, and I was able to close the door to the subconscious and open the conscious. This worked well, and the subject came back for consolation and was doing exceptionally well.

## Sexual Problems

A subject came in who had become unable to respond to her husband. She had been able to in the past. She wanted to again but couldn't. She relived a situation where she had been having sexual dreams about a close male friend. She started to avoid the friend and began acting as if they were having an affair. Her actions around their friend caused her husband to become suspicious. Her husband came home early, probably to check up on her and asked to have sex. She was busy fixing dinner and said no. He accused her of having sex with their friend.

During the argument, her husband said, "Well, I guess you give it to him, but not me." She was already feeling guilty because of the dreams, she overacted and became very angry and replied, "If that's the way you want it, that's the way it is." This angry statement went straight into the subconscious, and this blocked her ability to respond to her husband. The incident was relieved and removed, and the problem was solved. Don't say things in anger because the subconscious may cause the conscious to obey them.

A lot of problems relate to sex and the prevailing attitudes are about sex. The problems of sexual relations are created in great part by human nature and repression of sexual desires.

## Homosexuality

Some persons are born with latent homosexual tendencies and are not always aware that they have those feelings. They may have unexplained spells of depression or headaches and other mental disorders. It relieves some of the problems this creates when they find out and have time to adjust.

In my limited experience, hypnosis is no help for those because it is not an illness. Those that make a choice or are forced to participate in homosexual activities for different reasons, such as prison or unavailability of heterosexual partners can choose not to participate and may be helped.

A staff sergeant was married for several years and had two children. His problems were that when under stress, he would freeze up and would have to be physically removed from whatever he was doing. He had headaches, extreme nervousness, anger, and several other symptoms. I hypnotized him but wasn't able to help him. I sent him in for a psychiatric evaluation, and they found he was a latent homosexual. When he was able to accept this, he was able to deal with it. The service discharged him.

The other person went AWOL and slit both wrists before we were able to find out what was going on. When we inventoried his belongings and read his letters, it showed his worry about his feelings were more than he could accept.

Now I know you don't really want to read about other people's sexual problems. Most of you have enough of your own. I will say that anything that a person can think of has happened. Just remember there is help available, and life is what you say it is, no more and no less.

Sexual desire is one of the most, if not the strongest, motivation in the human race and begins at a very early age. Societies say to a young person, "Don't have sex until you are married and don't get married until you are twenty-one years old or finish your education." All this at an age when desire is creating the greatest confusion, and it frightens most parents so badly that most don't have any idea how to handle the situation.

Parents look at their own experiences and mistakes, fears and guilt and become determined to see that it doesn't happen to their children. This doesn't happen to everyone, but it sends many children and adults to doctors. Most adults judge themselves too harshly and feel that they made too many mistakes. Everyone has to deal with the guilt that builds up over time, and some don't know how to cope. Life is about making and learning from mistakes.

All illnesses can reoccur with the same symptoms but for a different reason. You may feel that the treatments haven't worked. You may just have a new cause for the problems like having a bad cold, curing it, and catching another cold. Most medications given for emotional problems reduce the symptoms but do not cure the problem.

Most doctors don't use hypnosis because of money and time, it takes about an hour for each hypnotic session, and a medical doctor can see several patients in an hour. After all, being a doctor is a business; and like any business, bills have to be paid.

Most doctors will not refer a patient to a hypnotist, but then they also don't want to refer you to another doctor. They might send you to specialists for a specific problem, and the specialists will send you back, and the doctor won't lose your business. If a doctor tries to hypnotize a patient and couldn't, he could lose the patient's trust and business. I had a doctor in a clinic I was working in told me that we were going to go broke if I didn't stop curing patients so fast, he was serious; after all, he had to pay the bills.

We had a discussion about this, and I stated that I would never treat a subject more than I felt necessary; this was one of the reasons I stopped working with him.

A doctor and friend lost his job in a private hospital because he wasn't putting enough patients into the hospital for treatment. The American Psychiatric Association didn't recognize hypnosis as a viable treatment; they may now.

Despite what you see on TV a few years ago, most psychiatrists wouldn't use hypnosis or would not admit to using it. I wonder why they had a couch. Sorry, I didn't mean to get off on a rant about doctors.

The conscious mind has a natural fear of change even if what it is doing is not working very well. Some subjects are willing to do almost anything to prevent changing what is causing their problems. If a hypnotist starts a personal relationship with a subject, he will not be able to successfully treat the subject's mental problems. Some subjects have a very deep need to believe that they are in total control.

I was in a class entitled "I'm OK, You're OK," and after we all introduced ourselves, a lady came up to me during a break and said that she was thinking about suicide because everything was going so bad in her life. I asked her if she was a religious person, and she said, "Yes." I said that the bible says that God said that he would never give her more than she could bare, and I suggested to her that she should turn all her problems over to God and just continue to do the best she could. She did and later told me that she was at peace with herself and doing fine.

I might add that a patient can also misuse hypnotism and lie to the hypnotist.

## Phobias

These conditions are characterized by intense fear of an object or situation which the patient consciously recognizes as no real danger to him, but once the fear starts, it will continue until the object or situation is gone. They are generally triggered by something of which the patient is unaware. These are irrational fears that can create repulsion, horror, and nightmares. They can be triggered by anything. The subject may think he knows what causes his reaction, but that is never the case. He may recognize the situation, not the trigger.

A subject came in with a fear of crickets. Crickets are like a small grasshopper. They can't physically hurt you. The subject was from England and was working in Texas as a nurse where there are a lot of crickets. She was going back home because she couldn't stand the sight of crickets. To emphasize her fear, this fear could be equated to a fear of lions, snakes, or some other deadly animals.

When she seen a cricket anywhere she lived, stayed, or even visited, even on a sidewalk, she could not ever go back to that area again, and she was running out of any place to go.

She relived an incident that happened in England when she was a young girl; she had a pet rabbit. She got a job that required her to be gone from home and also required a lot of study to learn the work. She had asked a younger brother to take care of her pet, but he didn't do it, and the pet was neglected for sometime.

She didn't know it, but the pet had been sick, and she went to check on it. When she opened the door, a swarm of large flies called blue bottle flies flew out into her face, and her pet was dead. She panicked and went into hysterics.

The crickets were acting as triggers to recreate the reactions she experienced by the death of her pet. After reliving and removing the incident, she was cured. When she came to see me again, she had a surprise for me and laid a live cricket on my desk which she was carrying in her bare hand.

## Claustrophobia

A fifty-five-year-old male with severe claustrophobia (fear of enclosed places) had the problem as long as he could remember. While under hypnosis, he went back and relived the incident that caused it. He went back to his birth. He had almost been crushed to death during delivery. When that suppressed incident was relived and removed, he was cured.

He came back to thank me and said, "If you never help anyone else, you have more than justified what you are doing by what you have done for me. You have taken me out of the deepest darkest, crushing situation and sat me on top of a beautiful sun-lit mountain."

It was a very nice thing to hear.

## Insomnia

A female came in who was unable to sleep. During the interview, she said that her husband was dead; and when I said that I was sorry to hear that, she stated, "Don't feel sorry, I killed the SOB."

He was trying to kill her and knocked her down, she grabbed a poker and hit him and killed him. He had a will that directed how he wanted to be buried. He wanted to be put into a crypt located in a lighted area and put in feet first.

She relived an incident in which she had him buried head first in a dark, damp corner of the crypt. Although he had kept her a prisoner in a private sanatorium for years and attempted to kill her, she apparently felt guilty and would see his face every time she tried to sleep. This incident was removed, and she reported she was sleeping well.

You may be totally justified for an action, but because of the way your conscious has been trained, you may still have to deal with guilt.

## Age Regression Technique

Here is a method used for all types of problems.

A hypnotist can direct a subject to go back to the time and/or place that caused his problem. He should be careful not to suggest that the subject go into a past life but just to return to whatever time and place that caused the problem as it could have been very recent. More often than not, the emotional experience is not a past-life experience but has happened in this lifetime. It's handled in the same way as past-life experiences.

When you read or see a movie about past-life experiences, remember that a hypnotist can produce all those types of experiences, and the subject could be told that they are real when remembered after they are awake. This should never be done. Very few incidents ever need to be remembered after the subject is awakened.

The subject is commanded that he will relive the incident that caused his problem and tell the hypnotist what he sees, feels, etc. He will relive the incident that caused the problem, the trigger that sets off the problem can be identified and removed, and with nothing left to trigger it, the problem will be gone.

The subject may start to talk in a foreign language or use terms that the hypnotist doesn't understand.

The hypnotist can command the subject to speak in a language that they understand. The hypnotist is not limited in the way he communicates with the subject.

The hypnotist shouldn't be concerned if it's real, imaginary, or a lie, as long as it helps the subject deal with his problems; after all that's what he gets paid for. You usually can tell if a subject is making something up. If a problem still exists, then the trigger was not found or another trigger is there, and you have to go back until all the triggers are removed.

He can have the subject deal with a situation creating guilt. He can have him ask for and accept forgiveness if that's required and remove the incident from the subject's mind and never to return and cause problems again.

I had a subject asked me how I knew if she was telling me the truth. I said it was her money, and if she wanted to lie, that was OK with me but might be a waste of her time. Sometimes subjects need to lie.

For every command given to a subject, there have to be several commands given to protect the subject from the original command. Here is an example: "You will stop smoking." Now the hypnotist should command the subject, "It will not make you overeat or nervous, and you will continue to command yourself that you will never want to smoke again."

Depending on the depth of sleep, commands may become less effective over a period of time and need to be reinforced.

## Coping Methods

There are good and bad coping methods. The good ones don't cause us problems. Some were started for a temporary problem and just became bad habits.

The list of bad ones covers just about everything and can be major ones that can threaten our lives. Every day the human mind has to cope within a rapidly changing environment. This is what the conscious learns to do from birth to survive. The way the subconscious mind works is, when the subject tells it to do something a few times, it gets programmed to do that until it is reprogrammed. It will influence the conscious to carry out the commands it has received and will continue to do so automatically. The result is it doesn't want to do it, and the subject fakes a headache or something else. The subject doesn't have to do it because the conscious mind is no longer in control, and it happens automatically. The subject's conscious mind becomes a victim of a bad direction. This is a bad coping method gone out of control.

In most areas where bad coping methods are developed, they can be removed, and there are many others. Migraine headaches, backaches, and stomach problems are some of the most common problem areas.

How is the subject going to cope with not doing the things he doesn't want to do when that crutch has been removed? The hypnotist has to install a method to handle a better way of handling situations when there are things he doesn't want to do.

Parents unwittingly can cause this to develop by asking a child who has a problem, "What's the matter, don't you feel well?" "Are you sick?" This gives the child a perfect opportunity to make up an illness. They feel sick, what better way to handle it than to get a headache or stomachache. This is not always the case, but you would be surprised how often it happens.

Subjects have been known to have several emotional headaches going at one time being triggered by different suppressed emotions. A hypnotist should find all the triggers and remove the triggers that caused the headache(s). Find the one that is causing the greatest pain first so that the subject can tell that he is starting to feel better. The hypnotist should go back and check for other headaches.

I had one subject who gave herself asthmatic attacks as an excuse not to go to school. She lived with her grandmother, and she had told her that the family had asthma. She faked an attack and it worked. She did this several times for things she didn't want to do, and it became a command to the conscious to have an asthmatic attack. This is not to indicate that all asthmatic attacks are emotionally induced.

## Pain

Pain is a warning signal to a person's mind just as a smoke detector is a warning signal at home or a red light in a car. To completely remove pain is very dangerous unless you find and remove the cause because there has to be warning a signal if one expects to survive. A hypnotist should never remove pain until he has found the cause.

For example, a person comes in with a headache; the hypnotist removes the pain without finding the cause of the headache. It turns out that the subject has a tumor in his brain. It continues to grow and kills the subject because he is not feeling any warning pain.

He should have first found the cause of the pain, was it physical or emotional. If it was caused by some suppressed emotions, then he could remove the suppressed emotions and the pain would disappear.

Sometimes reliving the problems are emotionally intense, but fear and pain can be reduced to an acceptable level but should never be entirely eliminated because they are used to help recognize the problem. Pain will be eliminated when the problem is removed.

A subject came in with pains in his lower back and legs. He had a brain tumor removed and had a loss of equilibrium. He had had the nerves cut in his upper back to relieve the pain and was taking several drugs for pain. He had difficulty of setting down, and I had to help him and put him on his side to be able to hypnotize him.

His neurosurgeon had advised him not to use hypnotherapy. The subject responded extremely well to hypnotherapy, and he got out of the chair and was jumping from one foot to the other. I had to warn him to stop and installed a command to protect him. The subject had started going fishing and was still feeling well two months after treatments were stopped.

## *Fear*

A subject needed to have dental work done but was too afraid to have it done. I set him up as follows:

When he sat down in the dental chair, his jaws would become numb, and he would not feel any pain, but he could still answer the dentist's questions. He would go to the beach and watch girls playing volleyball. After he was awake, he would only feel enough pain to protect his mouth and have only enough bleeding to clean the wounds. During healing, feeling would return to normal. They removed six teeth in four hours. When he came out to the waiting room, he asked me how long he was in; and when I told him, he replied, "Ten minutes, and the girls were beautiful."

The human mind is always very ready to eliminate pain.

A subject needed to have hip replacement but was too afraid. Commands were given to allow her to have the operation. She said that she worked very well before, during, and after the operation. She was walking when she last came by to see me.

A subject may have a fear of water. You find the incident and remove the trigger then remove the incident and fear. Now install respect and understanding for the dangers of water; after all water can kill you.

For fear of fire, leave some respect for the dangers of fire. The hypnotist simply explains that yes, water and fire can kill you; but with proper preparation, it can be made safe.

I use the word *respect* instead of *fear* because *fear* can be such a disabling emotion.

# Chapter 3

## *Reincarnation*

When I started asking subjects to go back into their minds to find what caused their problems, I was surprised when they went into past lives. I'm basically a very cynical person.

I had many patients relive past-life experiences to find the cause of their problems without being directed to go into a previous lifetime. After several subjects did that, I decided to open up my mind to the possibilities.

At the time I was doing hypnotherapy, I didn't intend to write about these cases, or I would have asked many, many more questions. The reader must understand that most of this was new to me, and I didn't know what questions to ask and misunderstood some of the answers to my questions. I didn't tape record most of the histories and erased most of those that I did.

I have the utmost respect for Shirley McClain for her courage in helping to educate the world about the possibility of past-life experiences. The experiences she writes about could have been from her imagination, or they could be real. It took courage to do what she did. The people who make fun of her are doing a great disservice to mankind.

Be very careful if you watch a demonstration on past-life regression. It may be real or from the imagination, but you will most likely believe it. A subject can answer questions and add in details that will surprise you; and if you attempt to prove what they say isn't true, forget it because they have convincing answers for all questions. Why do I warn you to be careful? Because it might not be true, and that matters. What we believe determines who and what we are.

Some subjects want to know if they have lived a previous life because some things seem so familiar. The problem with that is that the subject may attempt to live in a past life in this life. The hypnotist should not let this happen. Unless it's causing a problem, leave it alone. Now as I have said before, this might be all the work of the imagination, but let me say that several subjects related past-life experiences to me.

Many subjects have taken me through past-life experiences that were quite detailed, including their death, burial, and where they went after observing their own burial and their rebirth into their present life.

After death, they went to a place called "somewhere." Here on earth, we refer to this as heaven. There they were met and made welcome by familiar spirits they had known before.

Later, they meet with the spirits from the Divine Intelligence for a period of orientation and are given a review of their past life. This is all done without accusations or feelings of guilt. They are shown where they had made wrong decisions in that past life, and the karma it created and what the right decision would have been for the lessons they were there to learn. They are given a review of different existences available to choose from to continue their development and are prepared for their next existence.

Now that's nice to know because this would mean your spirit chose the existence that you are now living in, your parents, the time and place, your sex, physical looks, level of intelligence, nationality, all of what you are.

There are other dimensions besides earth for different training. Karma may explain why some are born with all of their problems.

You have freewill to make the choices. It's up to you to make the right choice. Choose to accept what you are, and choose to be happy.

Since your spirit chose this present existence, I guess we might just as well stop complaining, relax, and make the best of it.

You may not believe this, but you were born a divine spirit and at one time had the powers of a son or daughter of God. If you think this is all a bunch of baloney, that's fine; at first I thought so to. It sure beats "one life" and then off to heaven or hell.

This may sound like predestination, but a life just gives us the opportunities to learn the things we need. We have to learn to take advantage of those opportunities.

I warn you that the following case may not be true and could be a product of the subject's imagination or a story that she read and adopted as her own. I will say that by reliving it and having it removed from her mind, it solved her problems related to her present life. This is not an attempt to prove reincarnation. There are many books about reincarnation. The questions I asked were not attempts to lead the subject, but some might say that all questions are leading. Everyone hears what they want to hear.

It is very difficult to communicate with a subject reliving a past-life experience, but I have studied the tape over and over and believe that I have translated it the way she presented it to me.

I do not use the subject's name. The wording is what she said, and how she said it. The subject adds in a lot of information without being asked. *Her words are in quotes.*

A subject came to the clinic for treatment for emotional anxiety problems. She was married and had two children. Her husband loved her very much, but she felt lonely and lost and was always looking for something that was missing in her life.

The subject relived a past-life experience in which her name was Susan Valerie Kate and was born in 1794 and lived in Charlotte, North Carolina. They lived in a plantation called Thompson Hall in Charlotte, North Carolina. She said, "The plantation had Negro house servants named Aunt Lussey; she raised me, Chester, Shaw, Tarrit, John, Larnie, and Ellen."

Her grandfather's name was August Kate., "He said he was named August because he was born in August," and her grandmother's name was Sarah. They lived in Charlottesville, Georgia, and had "burned to death in a fire."

"Mama wanted to go home, but she couldn't go because her time had come, and I was born." Papa is talking about going over the mountains to Tennessee, but he was afraid that Mama's mental condition would never allow him to leave.

"One time, I said that Papa was going to Charlotte. Mama had got away from her nurse named Ellen who took care of her mother and lived in her room." Mama said that I was an ungrateful child to live in a lovely town like Charlottesville and that I didn't even call it by the right name. 'I didn't understand,' Father said, 'you have to understand, Susan, Mama thinks we are somewhere else.' Father said I was never again to say Charlotte again to Mama because that upsets her.

"She went back to Charlottesville in her mind, and she never came back, lost in her world. Papa says that Mama misunderstands me. Papa talked of taxes when I asked him. He said, 'The worry of taxes is not for the mind and the head of a beautiful young lady.'"

Susan met Brian Canfield. He lived on the next plantation. "He dressed in a silk waistcoat and fitted britches. We would meet by the river in Charlotte. I married Brian Canfield in 1811 when I was seventeen, and we lived in the West wing of Thompson Hall."

Susan died in 1811 during birth of their baby. After she was dead and lying in her casket, she told me, "Brian came, and he takes my hand and kissed my hand. His eyes are blue. He turned my hand over and placed a small gold key in it and closed my fingers over it. He said, 'I'm giving you a key, and you have to find the lock.'" I misunderstood what Susan was talking about, and I told her to look around for a door. She said, "There's no door." I asked what the key was for. "It's a clock key." I asked what was hidden in the clock, she said, "Brian put the ring, a gold ring in the clock. The only clock we had is on the fireplace, on the mantle." Brian had taken her gold wedding ring from her finger and put it in a clock over the fireplace. The small gold key in her hand was for that clock. "My hands are very cold in the box."

When I asked if she had previous lifetimes, she replied, "I only know that in trying to bear a child that the Death Angle came for me because I had elevated that man to the plane of God. I had to go, we can't love each other more than we love God." The Death Angle, how did that occur? "He was standing at the foot of my bed with arms outstretched I could not refuse to go. I attended my own funeral, I tried to talk to Brian, but he couldn't hear me. My grandparents that died in the fire were there. I could feel Brian's tears on my face. He wanted to be with me. There was no way I could make him understand." I asked why she was born as Susan, she said, "To teach Brian how to love completely without reservation."

I asked her to read from her headstone. She read: "Beloved Wife Susan Valerie Canfield. Till we meet again. 1794-1811."

I asked where she went to after the funeral, she said, "I can go anyplace I want to." I asked what the name of the place she finally went to. "The name of the place I went to is called 'somewhere.' I was met there by those that I had known who had preceded me in death. We couldn't talk; we didn't have physical bodies but could communicate with thought waves. They were waiting; I wanted to be with Brian. Brian had to come to me."

I asked if she was there when Brian came. "I was there to help when he came but wasn't allowed to help him because the time wasn't right, and he no longer needed the help I could give. They said I would hinder his progress." I asked what they had told her to do in the next life. "They don't tell me what to do, the choice is mine. They think—I don't understand to grow. They said that I was to be the child of Grace and Larry to continue to grow in grace and knowledge."

I asked why she had to grow. "Because I had loved a man more than God in a way that doesn't make sense, to love God more than Brian. I don't love God less for finding Brian again. I think that because of God's generosity, he is letting me see this man again. The souls know about Christ. Yes, I'm a soul from down here."

I asked when she entered her present life. "My soul entered the baby's body when I was born again. We are here, and they are there." I asked her to look around and tell me what she sees in the "somewhere." "Whatever I want is here, things are here. The sun is making shadows of the leaves. There are people walking. Sometimes they will turn as though they can see me, they can't see me."

The above statements led me to think that the "somewhere" may be located here on earth. That makes sense to me because of all the spirits here on earth.

They said, "I would not be lonely." When asked who "they" were again, she said, "They were the same as I was. They were the trainers only." I asked if they were souls, she said, "If I'm a soul, they were souls. They said, 'To stop looking for Brian, when the next time comes, Brian will be there.' I am to understand what the needs and desires of my own physical body are not shameful, passion is tempered with compassion."

I asked if *they* knew of Satan, she said, "Satan is an evil presence. Don't let yourself be possessed of evil but to God." What is God? "God is the Keeper of us in the 'somewhere.'" What did *they* tell you that Christ was? "Christ was God incarnate. Eternity is the only time that Brian and I can share." I asked again who *they* were, and what their names were. She said, "They didn't talk to me anymore." I asked why we are born. "I know that we are here to help each other."

Susan said in a low voice, "Clyde shouldn't know." I asked what it was that Clyde shouldn't know. She said, "Clyde shouldn't know that he was Brian." I told her that I would be very honored to have been her husband, but I wasn't allowed to remember those things.

## My Interpretation

During treatment, the subject believed that I, her hypnotist, was Brian; and she had finally found Brian again. This enabled me to assist her to overcome her desire to be with Brian again. She insisted that I allow her to cater a dinner for the clinic. I felt that this would help her, and it was a very wonderful dinner.

When her trainers (they) had told her that "when the next time comes, Brian will be there." She chose to reincarnate into a new life because of her desire to reconnect with Brian. This *selfish* choice was delaying the development of her soul in this present life.

The subject was given the necessary commands to remove those memories from her mind and release her from those desires, so she could fully live in this lifetime and stop her constant search for Brian. The subject said, "I know now that Christ is the love of my life."

## Message from an Entity

During treatment, Susan started to speak to me in a different sounding voice. It was neither male nor female. I will refer to that as an "entity," and it said, "I have a message for you." This was the first time this happened; I was surprised and apprehensive and asked if it was sure that the message was for me, and it said yes. I said, "OK. What's the message?" The "entity" replied, "This patient will give you a bible and wherever you find the word *believe*, you are to change the word believe to trust." I asked why, and it said, "The word *believe* was a misinterpretation of the original meaning as it was first written. They say they believe but very few trust." I said, "OK. How will that help me?" It said, "You are studying the bible, and this will clear up some things that are hindering your understanding." I was curious how the "entity" knew that I was studying the bible, but let that pass.

I asked the "entity," "What is the difference between believe and trust?" and it said that "they believe but very few trust. Believe means that you believe that there is a God. It is different from trusting. just that all our fears, all trials and having faith means that all our needs will be supplied. Trust is having salvation."

The "entity" gave me an example, saying, "You can believe that a chair will support your weight, but you won't sit on it because you are afraid to try it. Our only chance is to trust." I asked if there was anything else, and the "entity" said no. Since we were using the subject's time, I said it could help me in her treatment. The "entity" said that I already knew what her problem was, and I was doing the right thing to stop the patient from trying to live a past-life experience in this lifetime as this was delaying her progress.

I asked the "entity" if I could contact it again if I need help with other subjects, and after a long pause, it said, "I don't know." I said, "All right, and thanks for the help."

I didn't tell the subject about any of this at that time because I wanted to wait and see what would happen. At the next appointment, the subject brought a beautiful white bible and said, "I don't understand why, but I have to give you this bible." She had worked hard and won the bible in a church contest, and the lettering on the cover and her name were in gold letters. I told her she didn't have to give me the bible, and she became very, very upset and thrust the bible at my face and said, "Take it."

I took the bible, and she was very relieved. She said she didn't understand why, but she didn't have any other choice.

I explained to her what had happened and told her that I would replace the bible with an exact copy. She said that she would rather have her bible back after I had changed the wording. I said that I would return it if I could, not knowing what might happen next with the "entity" if I returned it. I changed the wording in the bible, and it did give me a better understanding because to me, the difference in the meanings made a big difference. Later, I returned to her bible.

Susan started speaking in her own voice again. She had remained asleep during all this time.

A lady came in with excessive fears of fire, dogs, and horses. She relived a past life in which she was four years old in a wagon train that was attacked by Indians. She was badly burned (fire) and was taken hostage from a burning wagon and taken back to the Indian village. She was thrown to the ground and attacked by the camp dogs. The women beat the dogs away from her. She lived with the Indians for approximately ten years. During this time, the Indian horses bit and kicked her.

When the tribe was relocated to a reservation in Oklahoma from Texas during the winter, the soldiers were looking for people the Indians had taken captive. A lot of the tribe had frozen to death. The wind blew the blanket off her head, and the sergeant saw her blond hair and blue eyes. They sent her back to the fort near Abilene, Texas, and the sergeant and his wife adopted her. She died from a fever about three years later and was buried at the Fort.

Now this may have been a book that she read and made a part of her past, but when these things were removed from her mind, her fears were released.

A female with extreme fear of water relived a past-life experience in which she and her father was thrown from a motorboat. They were ran over by it, and they were both killed. Her present family wanted to buy a boat but wouldn't do so because of her extreme fear.

After the removal of the memories and when last seen, she reported that the family had bought a boat, and she was learning to water ski. She had also went to "somewhere" after her death and had similar experiences as Susan. Some details have been left out because you could write a complete book on some of them.

The important thing is that after reliving these and removing the triggers, she was able to live a more normal life. Were the stories true? I couldn't care less as long as by reliving them and having them removed, they were relieved of their problems.

Some persons can hypnotize others without ever knowing that they have done so, think about that. If you find yourself under control of someone and can't understand why you do things that you know you shouldn't and are being used and abused, your conscious mind may be asleep. You can also accidentally hypnotize yourself, sometimes causing auto or other accidents. Watching the lane dashes in the road can have a hypnotizing effect.

One subject came in, and I had a real problem finding out what his problem was. He appeared to be in a sleepwalking state. At first I thought he was on drugs. I found out that he had been involved in a group doing some relaxation techniques and experiments in séances.

It turned out that his conscious mind had been accidentally put to sleep and was never awakened properly, and he was operating out of his subconscious mind. I actually had to wake up his conscious mind and put it back into control. The conscious mind had lost a lot of time and had to be brought up to date. It was the most confusing case I ever had. He was very lucky that I was able to figure it out.

I had a student in a class in an aircraft maintenance school that wanted to quit smoking, and I told him that he could stop now, and it wouldn't brother him. Two weeks later, he said that he had stopped, and he felt great. He said that he had never been able to stop before. I told him that he had made a perfect score on all the tests. I asked him if he had been in jail or prison, and he said yes. I explained that he was highly susceptible to suggestions and should never make decisions until he investigated what might happen. I gave him an example of hypnosis by locking his hand to his desk, and he couldn't lift it until I released it.

I wouldn't teach someone else to be a hypnotist because it may be too dangerous for that person. A person should know and be prepared to accept the risks and responsibilities.

A young boy came in with muscular dystrophy. He was so stiff in all his joints that he could hardly walk. I was able to reduce the pain and recorded the Green Routine for him. This subject affected me very much; and a day later after I got home and relaxed, I suddenly started crying. It was sometime later that I was able to identify the cause.

A hypnotist should be aware of his own weaknesses and personal problems, and his ability to handle them because when treating a subject, he is looking into a mirror of his own personality. This can create more problems when presented to his conscious mind unexpectedly. How can you protect yourself, I don't really know, except to be aware of the dangers.

I have spent many hours crying with subjects as the details of their problems unfolded. Objectivity forgets that because a hypnotist has to become involved to understand and help. At least I did.

I do know that this hypnotist prays a lot for protection of the subject and himself. I didn't have a choice but simply had to become a hypnotist. I seem to know what to do once I got inside a subject's mind; maybe I have done this before in some past life, I don't really know.

Psychiatrists are required to go through analysis for their own protection before being board certified to practice.

A psychiatrist I know had been the president of the American Psychiatric Association at one time. He was removed as president because he had opened a hypnotic clinic. He once asked me, "Where does a hypnotist go to when he needs help?" After sleeping on the question, my reply was, "To God or another hypnotist if you can be hypnotized."

It's very difficult for a hypnotist to be hypnotized. I have always envied a person who is able to be hypnotized. There is so much help available by its use. It is a privilege to be associated with someone who can trust another human enough to be hypnotized.

# Chapter 4

## Self-Hypnosis

I practice self-hypnosis, and it is effective but takes longer to achieve results compared to being hypnotized by someone else. Using self-hypnosis relieves you of most of the dangers of hypnosis as you are in control and not by someone else. If you use self-hypnosis, be sure to set a time limit to wake up.

## The Green Routine

I developed the following routines to assist subjects to set goals and implant them in the subconscious. The best way to use this is to make your own tape recording and work on the things you need to change and listen to it when you go to bed.

Make the commands positive. You don't have to go to sleep for this to work. This is quite long, and as you get use to using it, you can shorten it. Find a quite place and make yourself comfortable, take your time.

Clear your mind and relax. The thought, sight, and sound of the word green will trigger your mind to follow the commands. Green is your magic word, green! This color will never cause you to do anything that would hurt you. It will only work to help you.

Ready, let's start.

Relax your body and concentrate on the center of your forehead, see it in your mind's eye. Green! Relax your mind and let it sleep and rest. Green! You feel tired and want to sleep, green! Sleep. Relax your mind and sleep. Deeper and deeper with breath, green! You will remain asleep until the time limit runs out. Or if you need to wake to take care of an emergency or something important, you will wake up and feel alert and able to do what you need to. Green!

Next, open a pathway of communication to the subconscious of your mind. Green!

You will visualize the color green, see it in your mind, and send it to the center of your brain. Green! Green! Now the path to the subconscious is open. Here is where you should add your commands to solve your own problems. Make them positive commands.

*The following commands are listed here as examples*:

You will hear my voice and will obey my commands. Green! Green! None of these commands will ever hurt you and can only help you. The commands will be released from the subconscious to assist you to accomplish your objectives. You will obey them. Green! Green! You will obey all commands unless they would be detrimental to your health. Green!

You will think of yourself as being healthy and full of energy. Visualize yourself standing in front of a mirror and see yourself as a healthy, happy person. Build the image. When you have it, lock it in your mind. Green!

You will control the pains in my body and allow only the necessary warning signs to warn and prevent them from damaging my health. Green!

You will concentrate on each area as directed and start the process necessary to heal my mind and body from the top of my head to the tip of my toes. Green!

Start at the top of the head and send green to the top of the head. Green! Heal my body!

Now send green to the head and relax and heal it. Green!

On down to the neck and shoulders. Green! Relax and heal. Take your time. Green!

Send green down the arms, down to the elbows, through the forearms to the hands, to the fingertips, and relax and heal them. Now send green into the chest and upper back and heal that area. Green! Heal these areas. Green!

Concentrate on the stomach and lower back, see them and send green into these areas and relax and heal them. Green!

See the lower abdomen and hips, send in Green and heal them. Green!

See the thighs, send green into them and work on healing the nerves and circulation as needed and heal. Green!

Next send green into the calves and ankles of the legs and heal them. Green!

Concentrate on the feet and toes and heal them. Leave only enough feelings to protect them. Green!

You will influence and direct all my eating and drinking habits to provide the proper nutritional needs of my mind and body. Green!

Now let's send a big wave of healing green from the top of the head all the way down and relax all areas and relax and rest. Each time see, hear, or think green, your commands will become stronger and have more effect until they become good habits.

Now at the count of three, you will wake up and feel normal and relaxed, seal all commands into the subconscious and obey them. You will be alert and normal or go into a normal sleep at night.

*One*, start waking up. Wake up.

*Two*, you will obey all commands and be fully awake at the count of three.

*Three*, wake up feeling wonderful and relaxed. Three green! Wake up and obey all the commands.

*Learn to use this, it will work.*

After I retired, I had a subject's husband call and asked me to go see his wife. She had been a subject of mine, and I had recorded the Green Routine for her. He had fallen off a roof and broke his back and was in a full body cast, she was in a hospital ward. She would stand at attention and said that the devil was in her room, and she would stand up until he left.

She would stand until she passed out. He said that the only time she seemed normal for a while was after she listened to my tape. I explained that I had retired, but if he could get her doctor's permission, I would go see her. Her doctors wouldn't give permission.

## Problems Being Hypnotized

Some very good subjects may not be ready to be hypnotized at that particular time and place or by that hypnotist or have too many other things on the mind. Don't ever feel that you are not a good subject or can't be hypnotized because under the right conditions, almost everyone can. Maybe your mind is saying that you shouldn't trust the hypnotist, or the conditions are not safe. Trust your instinct and go somewhere else, but don't let anything prevent you from using the opportunity to be helped.

I screened my subjects very carefully. I treated only people who want to be helped. I didn't work with a person who is suicidal as I didn't have the facilities to protect them during treatment.

One subject under treatment said that she was thinking about suicide. I installed a command that she didn't have the right or authority to do that. She took an overdose of sleeping pills; and just before she passed out, she called the clinic, and the nurse called an ambulance to take her to the hospital. When she came back to see me, she said that the doctors at the hospital were trying to get her to sue us. She said that just before she passed out, she had a clear picture of me telling her that she didn't have the right to kill herself, and that's when she call the clinic.

I don't treat people who make threats and are too aggressive; I have to protect myself. I don't treat people who are sent or forced to come in by their parents or others. Sometimes the person bringing someone in is the one needing treatment.

The subject's interview list is very complete, and questions are asked about every aspect of your life. The more information the hypnotist has, the better they can help you.

The initial discussion of a subject's problems has to be approached with diplomacy, gentleness, and patience. These are necessary, or they will not come back. Some people are shy, and it's best to let them bring up problems of a personal nature.

If you want to see one of the most beautiful sights ever seen, just look at a subject when they have had all of their hates, guilt, prejudices, fears, worries, pains, etc., removed and feel that they are safe and everyone loves them. They get such an angelic look about them that it will bring tears to your eyes. You might ask here, why not leave a subject in that state? The main reason I can think of is that they wouldn't have any protection from the rest of us, and they would be like a lamb among wolves.

They also must be allowed to live out their lives, be able to make mistakes, have experiences both good and bad, and learn and develop as God intended.

The situation that happened in Waco, Texas, is a good example of people being misled into believing they were going to paradise if they did everything they were told by their leader. I have asked many people if they would like to be put into that state of paradise, and I haven't found a volunteer yet. Wouldn't you think that everyone would want to be in paradise even for just a little while?

If you have tried giving yourself positive suggestions and it's not working for you, stop using the term *I* to give yourself commands or directions; use the word *you*, as if you are talking to another person. To most people, *I* is a negative path of communication in the brain, such as I don't want to, I don't like, I hate, etc. Command yourself like the old sergeant talking to a new recruit. Make all your commands positive, and you will see the difference. Did I say talk to yourself? Yes, I did. Direct and command yourself. You have the responsibility for yourself.

Life is nothing more or less than what you say it is. A hypnotist has to be aware that people have a tremendous imagination, and some problems are created by the imagination. Many people will try to tell you that your problems are just in your head; so what? It's still a problem, and just telling someone to forget it doesn't work. That's what they are already trying to do.

Subjects can make up stories that they might think the hypnotist wants to hear. All this has to be dealt with. It's a tough game out there. Any good doctor knows that some people are sick because it works for them. They may realize that it's a bad coping method, but it may be all they have.

It is very difficult for an individual to determine if they are addicted, and they usually believe that they can quit at any time they want to. You hear about this every day, and hypnosis can help but not always cure some very strong addictions. If you really want to find out if you are addicted, just quit for a couple of months.

Smoking is tied into everything in your life, even the good things. If you are trying to quit by yourself, don't tell yourself that smoking will make you sick. What will happen if you quit smoking and start again, you want to be sick? Do tell yourself that quitting smoking will make you feel better and will not make you nervous or irritable and will not make you overeat. Never tell yourself or anyone else that you still want to smoke.

You put yourself in a trick; you won't smoke, but you really miss and want it. Talk about self-abuse. Just go get a stick and hit yourself over the head, at least it will feel good when you stop. Tell yourself over and over again that you will never want to smoke again. The hypnotist may have cured your old addiction, and you have developed a new one.

I had a young man come in that was trying to get off cocaine and had become addicted to methadone. While he was under hypnosis, I reversed his symptoms. Whenever he took drugs, he went into withdrawal symptoms; and when he stayed off, he got an artificial high. This worked well, and he was doing fine. His father stopped treatment because of other problems in the family and moved the family to the Australian outback. Addictions may come on so slowly that you are there before you realize it.

One subject was an alcoholic because he had started to drink after he had fallen under an aircraft propeller during a compression check on an aircraft. During a check, the engine is being turned over by the starter and won't be started. He had always been afraid of propellers, and although the propeller just kicked him off the work stand, it scarred him so badly that he couldn't work if he wasn't drinking. This was ruining his marriage, and he was living out back of their house in a small house trailer.

After reliving the incident and having it removed from his mind, he was able to quit. The irony of this is that his wife had become involved in a relationship with another man and wanted a divorce. I asked her to come in to discuss the situation, and she did. I advised her that since the situation had changed, she might be wise to take more time to make a final decision especially since there were children involved. The last time I checked, they were still married. Sometimes curing a problem can create other problems that must be addressed.

Do you ever want to see your worst enemy? Look in the mirror. The person that lies to you the most will be looking back at you and does it so well that you don't even know it's a lie.

Most of my subjects were women. Most men won't seek help with their personal problems. They won't ask for directions when driving either. Well, I have hundreds of case histories that cover the whole scope of human problems, but I think this is enough for you to see how this works.

I have had subjects that start to cry, scream, kick holes in the wall, and fight to escape what's happening as they start to relive the incidents. The hypnotist has to be ready to protect the subject and defend themselves at all times. He can control the intensity of the emotions, but sometimes they happen pretty fast; and since you don't know what is going to happen, you have to be ready. Is it a lot of fun? No, because the incidents are never good or pleasant, or they wouldn't have created the problems.

Use hypnosis but protect yourself.

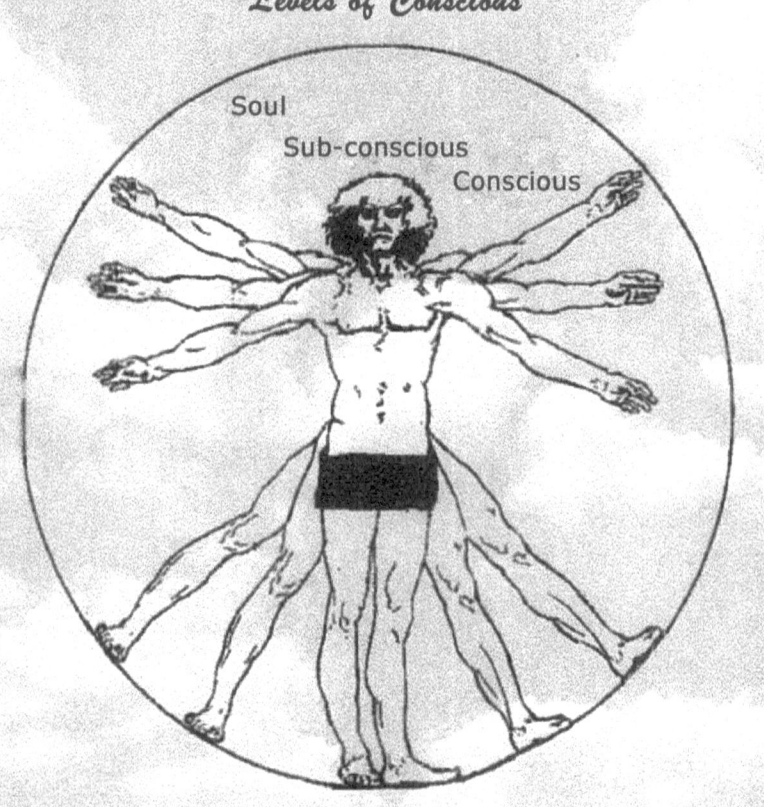

Levels of Conscious

Soul

Sub-conscious

Conscious

# Chapter 5

## *Levels of Consciousness*

There are several levels of consciousness that the human mind can experience each day. To understand the human mind, I divide it into three main levels: the soul, the subconscious, and the conscious. Down through the eons of time and evolutions of generations, we are all children of God engaged in the development of the spirit.

The human mind works like a computer. The soul is the basic program. The subconscious is the memory, and the conscious is the program added during a lifetime. The human body is much like a robot that carries out the programs of the computer. Like other computers, the human brain operates on a small amount of electricity; the amount does not remain at a fixed frequency. This current can vibrate rapidly and at times very slowly. Scientists have divided the frequency spectrum into four different segments based on the cycles per second (cps).

* Beta is above 14 cps when the body and mind are alert and active.
* Alpha is from 7 to 14 cps, and it is associated with light sleep and dreaming.
* Theta is from 4 to 7 cps, and it is associated with deeper sleep and is used with hypnosis and painless surgery.
* Delta is below 4 cps, and it is the deepest sleep. In hypnosis, this is referred to as somnambulistic sleep.

This book is primarily concerned with the existence of spirits/souls in the physical existence.

## Spirits/Souls

### The Spirits

In the beginning, all spirits were created in the image of the Creator. Spirits, being a part of God, are immortal and never cease to exist. The destiny of the spirit is to become one with the Divine Intelligence we called God.

Spirits are created by God to be his companions and are referred to as the "Sons of God," and being children, they have limited power of God but not the intelligence and knowledge of how to use that power.

After spirits complete their development and become a part of the Divine Intelligence (God), they still have freewill and may choose to take on other tasks; and some become angels or teachers to assist other spirits. Spirits may choose to return to the earth dimension and can create problems that may have to be worked through.

God did not dictate to his children what they would do and gave them freewill, and as all children do during development, they can make errors in judgment and don't always use their powers as their father intended.

The earth dimension was created for all the species for their development. There are *free spirits* that have completed their development and *entrapped spirits* that are the result of spirits choosing to unite with the "Daughters of Man."

*Free spirits* have the power to project into and leave the earth dimension. They may choose to use the human species as one method for their development and enter into a body shortly before or after birth and remain as long as they deem necessary.

### Entrapped Spirits

In the Old Testament of the King James Bible, spirits choose to unite with the daughters of Adam and Eve. This union created children containing both spirit and soul. We are the children of that union. These spirits are entrapped until they accept Christ as their savior.

There are old spirits and new spirits. Old spirits have had more than one incarnation and have had past-life experiences. New spirits are starting their process of development through degrees of awareness and do not have past-life experiences.

Spirits can continue to make the same mistakes over and over again even though that can delay their development. These mistakes are called *karmic debts* and must be worked through by the spirit. Making mistakes is a learning process if we learn from them.

The lessons and experiences, both good and bad, learned in a lifetime are retained in the spirit's memory when a spirit leaves the human mind.

Spirits may choose the gender, type of family, nationality, location, physical characteristics, and disabilities using past karma to select a soul's personality necessary for its development.

One of the reasons the spirit chooses the earth existence is to learn to overcome self or maybe a better term is selfishness. Some people refer to this as the ego.

When God gave spirits the use of the human species, he required that spirits work within the limitations of the human physical body and mind. These limitations are necessary to protect spirits from themselves. If they had unlimited power, new developing spirits could damage themselves because of the lack of training of how to use that power.

The memories that are retained by the spirit are not normally remembered when it reincarnates. If it does remember, it seems to disappear after a short time after birth. The conscious mind is not aware of these spirits, except in unusual circumstances.

It is important to remember that the spirit may influence the soul but cannot dictate to it except in emergencies, but it also has the power to influence the soul when the soul is awake, and this can cause a conflict between the soul and spirit when the soul tries to ignore positive messages it receives from the spirit through the subconscious.

## Karma

Karma is the accumulation of past experiences of the spirit's development. Spirits use karma to develop the human personality for an earth existence. The personality contains the necessary elements needed in a lifetime in order for the spirit to develop and help it become a member of the Divine Intelligence. Spirits can use as many lifetimes as necessary. Time does not exist in the spiritual dimension. It can create bad karma by selfish decisions. This is not about petty mistakes but things that delay the Spirit. Some of the karma is not very pleasant to have come back and relive and make some sort of restitution or do something to receive forgiveness.

Karma may help explain to some people why they are in the situation they find themselves in. Your spirit may be using you. Hypnosis cannot resolve karmic debts—those must be worked through by your Spirit—but it may be used to help you understand why you are here.

## *Souls*

The Christian bible states that man was created from the dust of the earth. He was put here to tend the Garden of Eden and created Eve from Adam's rib. That creation was the Adam and Eve referred to in the bible.

Soul/Conscious represents who and what we are. It starts out at birth with limited intelligence and is developed through experience and training. The soul has the ability to think and live a life of its own independent of a spirit. It usually considers itself as the only level and attempts to act as God.

To protect itself, a soul may split the conscious into several different personalities to handle extreme situations that one type of personality can't handle, and they can be in conflict with each other and may switch with each another.

The duality of occupation of the human mind is very difficult for the soul (us) to understand especially if we end up in prison or die a slow torturous death or have to live in extreme pain in an ugly deformed body and can't figure out why this is happening through no fault of our own.

When hypnotized, the conscious part of the soul's mind is inactive unless directed to be involved. Souls are destined to die, and we have to trust in God that this is meaningful and necessary. The physical body is an aspect of the soul. When it has served its purpose, it is released and returned to dust.

The soul is not perfect and has selfish desires and emotions and very limited intelligence and physical abilities when compared to some other species. When the soul/conscious is awake, it screens information going into the subconscious mind, but the soul's conscious mind can be distracted or put to sleep, and information and commands can be installed into the subconscious to help the conscious overcome problems.

The soul is able to change its programming by hypnosis or repetition of commands and to assist the spirit attain what it needs, but it must be sure that it only implants suggestions to assist and change only the areas that are causing problems. Even though a spirit is using the same body, it is not dictating to us. The soul still has the responsibility to think and make good decisions.

There is no proof to us that the spirit or subconscious exists. We are only aware of the conscious mind that we use in our everyday activities. The lack of proof to the conscious mind to us that the spirit's existence causes us to question the existence of God.

On the positive side, after sufficient development, a spirit/soul may get to enjoy all the experiences of a wonderful lifetime with love of family and friends.

## Subconscious

This level of the mind is used as a two-way channel of commutation between the spirit and the soul/conscious. It acts as a memory for the spirit. It is programmed to sustain us until the soul's conscious mind learns to do it.

The subconscious mind does not judge whether changes are good or bad for you. That's why you have to be careful about what you try to change because the subconscious mind is waiting for directions to help create what it is directed to do. The spirit and the soul are supposed to make those judgments. If you can't change it, it may be karma, and you have to accept it.

Statements are made with intense concentration, such as anger should be avoided because you are not thinking rationally and can drive the command into the subconscious. Don't ever say that if certain things happen, you will kill yourself; the subconscious may cause it to happen. So be very careful what you tell yourself to do especially when angry. The subconscious never sleeps and is waiting for instructions. When the soul/conscious is asleep, the subconscious can be used to recall and relive past-life experiences.

## Suicide

God did not intend that a soul interfere with the spirit's learning progress. This is the ultimate selfish act. Taking your own life is very damaging to the spirit and apparently requires much longer for the spirit to recover and continue its progress. Under normal conditions, spirits can reincarnate as soon as they are ready; and as we gauge time, about one hundred years is about average. This amount of time eliminates confusion with other persons who knew them.

## Conclusion

Most of what we know about the spirit and soul is a theory. We humans are not allowed to know for certain how this works. I say the following with the greatest humility because I'm in the same boat as you, unless your development has reached the stage ready to consider the above information, you may not believe any of the above. If you are trying to make sense of this life, this will give you something to think about and this may help you.

If you worry about these things, stop and enjoy your life; after all, this life is nothing more or less than what you tell yourself it is. Love one another.

## *Subliminal Messaging*

Subliminal messaging is used primarily to influence our thinking patterns. A signal or message is embedded in another object, designed to pass below the soul's conscious limits of perception. These messages are indiscernible to the conscious mind but are perceptible to the subconscious mind, for example; an image transmitted so briefly that it is perceived subconsciously but not otherwise noticed.

Subliminal techniques may be used in advertising and propaganda and may sometime be used to make us purchase items that we otherwise might not want or need.

A study was made concerning drink and food in a movie by quickly flashing the slogans "Drink Coca-Cola" and "Eat Popcorn" for 1/3000 of a second at five-second intervals. Popcorn and Coke sales increased 57.5 percent and 18.1 percent respectively. The Federal Communications Commission (FCC) released a policy statement in 1974, claiming that such messaging was "against the public good." I do not believe that stopped their use.

This may explain why people are found with their houses full of worthless, unneeded items. When questioned, they say "I don't know why I got all these things." The only protection we have from subliminal messaging is to investigate what we think and buy more carefully.

If the conscious becomes too strong or cynical and chooses to input to the subconscious that would create karma and seriously damage the spirit, free spirits have the option of overriding or leaving the conscious. It's important to control your sleeping environment because all sorts of unwanted information can enter the subconscious while the guard is sleeping.

The intention of why we do things is very important. Every action and change in your experiences reflects an intention. You create your reality with intentions. Make all thoughts for actions with unselfish intension.

Remember, you have free choice and can make good choices and bad choices. Choose to make good choices.

# Chapter 6

## *Emotional Control*

The following information is not intended to create a person unable to react with emotions appropriate to the situation. The lack of emotional control causes more problems than anything else in our mental makeup. We seem to encourage excessive emotions in our society. Programs and methods must be developed to accomplish control.

Before we can learn how to control the emotions, we have to define what emotions are and identify what causes them. Emotions are reactions to stimulus from or to the mind or body. All emotions can be misused and cause us problems with devastating results if they become excessive and can cause hysteria or depression and can happen unexpectedly.

Don't think that your likes and dislikes are permanent. They can be changed with the snap of the fingers.

I put on a demonstration for a group on the control of love and hate, like and dislike.

A young lady was the subject, and I told her that when I snapped my fingers, she would love her husband so much that she couldn't stay away from him; and when I said apples, she would hate him so much that she would want to hit him, but couldn't. When I said apples, she wouldn't have anything to do with him. He asked what he had done, and she said, "You know what you've done!" I snapped my fingers, and she was all over him like a warm blanket.

Excessive emotions create excessive adrenaline. These create a feeling of exhilaration and excitement, but when they burn out of your system, you will go into a depression, just as low as the high was from normal. Anger creates instant adrenaline high and can become addictive.

A subject was getting depression and migraine headaches every day. Every day he would find something to get angry over. I developed a "plus ten, minus ten" chart with the burnout time to help judge his highs and lows. He was addicted to adrenaline and was using anger to get it. If he got to an eight high by 10:00 a.m., he went down into an eight-low depression headache by 3:00 p.m. unless he became angry again. With a little work, he controlled it to a plus or minus two, no depression or headaches.

There is an old saying: "When emotions take over, good judgment and common sense go out the window." Emotional reactions can be either positive or negative depending on the response of the individual. The emotions that create healthy and happy feelings such as, love, happiness, devotion, loyalty, respect, and friendship are referred to as being positive. When used properly, they will develop a well-rounded personality. The people you meet that have pleasant personalities have learned to control their emotions.

The emotions that create unhealthy physical and mental reactions are referred to as selfish negative emotions. Most of the problems created by these emotions may be helped by hypnosis. They are anger, hate, depression, jealously, guilt, and greed to name just a few. These create reactions that cause us problems. The effect of these can make changes that are detrimental to our minds and bodies. These are the ones that we need to learn to control, or they will control us.

## Children

We must teach children how to use reactions or limit, stop, or prevent those that harm us from happening. There are few schools that train us to control our emotion. The public schools no longer allow teachers to discipline students. What training we get is usually from those who don't have very good control of their own emotions and their reactions from what upsets or annoys them.

Training should begin at the preschool level. Negative reactions can be used to assist us if we learn how and when to use them.

The emotion of anger is a good example. Anger causes the mind and body to prepare to defend itself if attacked by removing the blood from the extremities and increases the blood flow and adrenaline to the brain to increase awareness, and it gives you increased strength and quicker reaction time.

Excessive fear can also cause panic and paralyze us. We need to know how to create and control anger when we need it and prevent it when we don't.

Hate is one of the most debilitating emotions of all because it affects all other aspects of your life. To free yourself of hate of another person, you must forgive that person. That person may never know that you forgave them, but it frees you. To forgive is very difficult because it goes against your ego and pride, and anger and hate give you a false high of feeling good.

Children are born totally dependent on others. They are programmed to be totally selfish for survival. They learn early what their parents react to and will use whatever works to get what they need, and they are born with different needs. They are limited on how to express themselves. Parents have to learn what those needs are and how to fulfill them.

A child's subconscious mind never sleeps and records everything it sees or hears 24 hours a day. It cannot judge what is good or bad even in an adult. The conscious mind learns to judge what is good or bad when it is awake.

There are a multitude of books on parenting children. Check them out and use the ones used by other parents that work for them. Start teaching them emotional control as soon as possible. Every time something is done right, reward that child with inputs of praise, love, hugging, etc. Don't ever use food as a reward.

A child does not understand the inflicting of pain to train at an early age. The feelings of pain are known only to a child to tell them when something is wrong with their bodies, and they are programmed to avoid it. Don't use food to alleviate pain.

The following information is not intended to create a person unable to react with emotions appropriate to the situation.

Never display disagreements in front of children. Treat all children with the same loving care and attention, and respect and ensure that they treat each other the same way.

It is the parents' responsibility to know what their children are doing 365 days, 24 hours a day; what's in their computers, rooms, cars, and where they go; and who they associate with.

Children must earn your trust and privacy. Nobody ever said that it's easy being a parent. Young children make mistakes in judgment, and it can be especially devastating for girls that get pregnant out of wedlock; that's when they need the family's love and understanding the most. The mistreatment of children is one of the most stupid, selfish acts an adult person can commit.

Talk to your subconscious, its listening; and give it directions for what you want to happen. Use the green routine, record them, make them positive, and listen to them in your sleep. Be firm, say "You will obey my commands," such as, "You will accept what has happened. Be happy and move on with your life." Did I say "Talk to yourself? Yes! Put yourself in charge. Your life is what you say it is, no more and no less. A little positive thinking. Yes.

## Television

About every ten years, hypnotism becomes popular again. Television and movies are starting to show hypnotic induction on the screen. Both may create hypnotic trances especially in children and suggestible persons, and the information can go directly into the subconscious. This is very dangerous because many programs do not go through the proper procedure for waking up.

Most programs are sponsored by commercials, and some people are induced to purchase things they don't need or even want. About 75 percent of all TV is commercials.

Some children's educational programs are very good and are good training tools. Limit the amount and type of TV viewing. The less TV that we see the better, for what you experience through the five senses have a profound effect on who and what we are, especially young children when their conscious mind is being formed. Don't put a child in front of a TV to act as a babysitter. Don't leave the TV on at night when sleeping because the subconscious mind never sleeps. Do not install TV in the bedroom. Some TV programs are for adults only. Use lockout features on those programs.

Children watching TV from the time they are born see violence, mayhem, rape, murder, robbery—just to name a few—that are drilled into them day after day, night after night, 24 hours a day. Adults have been seeing these things all their lives, and we are seeing the negative results of these as they bring these things in their lives.

Some information has effect on the unborn children. I was in movie with a lady who was seven or eight months pregnant. We were watching a movie about earthquakes. They had installed very large speakers for this movie. When the sound became very loud, the baby started kicking her so hard that she had to leave the movie. After the baby was born, he panicked at every loud noise.

I'm going to share something with you here that have taken me over seventy years in this life to learn. I believe that one of the main reasons we are here in this dimension at this time is *"to learn to become totally unselfish."* Don't try to judge whether an action is unselfish or not because you cannot, just try. Christ should be our example. This life might just be another type of school.

The truth is, you can't be happy and contented by staying totally within yourself. There is no true happiness in there for you. Whoever wrote those books on taking care of number one didn't know what they were talking about.

A person should take care of him or herself, yes, but do it for the right reason, an unselfish reason. I add this here because most of the problems a person have are created by some selfish reasons. I have found that all negative emotions are selfish. When you stop thinking about yourself, you will find happiness and remember that a person cannot insult you without your permission.

This might explain some of your present problems, and if all of this doesn't scare the hell out of you, it should. All the information is true, at least to my knowledge.

I have had experiences with "entities" of unknown origins who have advised and helped me. The information received was welcomed and appreciated. Don't be afraid to talk to those "entities" that may contact you; just be cautious. So far none have been evil.

Everyone has a *guardian spirit* to help, assist, and protect them. When you feel that something is not right, that may not just be your training but may be your *guardian spirit* trying to help. Trust and act on those feelings. This is one of the reasons that we sleep before making a big decision.

I personally feel that I am receiving help in writing this book and keep revising it. I always assumed that everyone had common sense, but I have found that is not true. I don't know how one attains common sense except through heredity or experience and the input from other senses, but there seems to be far less of both as time goes on.

People seem to have less real meaningful experiences with TV and computers keeping us occupied. Well, have a wonderful life and love one another.

# Chapter 7

## *Questions and Answers*

Q. If you learn of a crime, should you report it to the law?
A. No, I wouldn't stand up in court anyway.

Q. What is the hypnotist's responsibility to the subject?
A. Total responsibility while under treatment.

Q. What if it seems a subject should really suffer for something, should a hypnotist just let him suffer?
A. No, the hypnotist cannot judge others.

Q. What gives the hypnotist the right to make decisions for a subject?
A. The subject.

Q. Who does the hypnotist owe his loyalty to?
A. The subject.

Q. If what you say is true, why does the hypnotist seem to have problems or illnesses?
A. Some hypnotists can help themselves with self-hypnosis but some cannot, and I don't know why, except I believe that hypnotists may need to experience problems in order to help others. It is my belief that everyone basically has the same types of problems, and the difference between them is in the matter of intensity.

One of the dangers to a hypnotist is that he is looking into a mirror of his own emotional problems and is not always able to recognize them and protect himself.

Q. Can a subject be forced to have sex under hypnosis against their will?

A. Here I have to beg the answer as I have never attempted this, but it would never be necessary to force anyone to have sex if that was what a hypnotist wanted to do. When a subject is asleep, the hypnotist can give the subject commands at a trigger word, say, a snap of the fingers. The subject will see the hypnotist as his or her spouse or someone that he or she wishes to have sex with. The hypnotist would then appear as if he or she is actually that person to the subject. Therefore, for the subject to have sex with the hypnotist would not be the fault of the subject. It would certainly be rape by the hypnotist just as for a doctor or dentist using drugs to rape. Remember, protect yourself at all times.

Q. What are past-life experiences?

A. These are usually not believed in Christian areas of the world. Most of the rest of the world's societies believe in past lives and reincarnation in one form or another.

Q. Can a subject be hypnotized without his consent?

A. *Yes*, they can be hypnotized without their consent or knowledge. Pretty scary stuff, yes? Also, a person's normal sleep can be entered into, and they may be taken into a hypnotic sleep. Don't worry too much because most likely no one wants to put you to sleep anyway.

Q. Why have I stopped doing this professionally?

A. It is because of the possibility of being sued and the lack of insurance and understanding and people's fear about hypnosis. How would you answer some redneck judge as to why you were even doing this? Do you believe he would accept the answer?

Q. Last of all, why me? Why was I compelled to get into this?

A. The only reason for doing this work was to help the subjects every way I could. I was receiving payment to help, not to hurt, not to punish, and most of all, not to judge. Not to judge is one of the most difficult things to follow.

Aren't we all prostitutes of one sort or another? We all sell our time, knowledge, and skills to someone. You know, God doesn't have a voice or a body to do his work, and sometimes he gives someone the ability to help others. If God allows subjects to come to me for help, I will do everything God will allow me to do to help them; and if God doesn't want them helped, he needs to keep them away from me.

My hope is that by telling the truth about hypnosis, it will help prevent its misuse. My advice is to use it when needed and protect yourself at all times.

Well, have a nice day and start treating yourself and others with respect. If you don't, you may have to come back and do it again. The next time, you may be mistreated as you have mistreated others.

I hope you enjoyed my story and maybe have some new things to think about. I think that some of the things I've experienced may answer some of your questions.

## *The End*

# References

Michael R. Hathaway. *The Everything Hypnosis Book.*

Karen Armstrong. *A History of God.*

Gary Suave. *The Seat of the Soul.*

Michael D. Coogan. *The Illustrated Guide to World Religions.*

Edgar Cayce. *There Is a River.*

www.ingramcontent.com/pod-product-compliance
Lightning Source LLC
Chambersburg PA
CBHW061221280526
45784CB00006B/2577